The Little Wire Hanger In The Closet

Written by
Isreba Wheeler
AKA
Hope Syndreamz

Illustrations by
Sky Owens

The ongoing saga of Life's lessons through the eyes of a young boy

#3

The Little Wire Hanger in the Closet
Published by Dumplinz Book Publishing
BRONX, New York
(917) 642-5549
hopesyndreamz@optonline.net
www.dumplinzbookpublishing.com

ALL RIGHTS RESERVED

No part of this book may be reproduced or transmitted in any form or by any means—electronic or mechanical, including photocopying, recording or by any information storage and retrieval system without written permission from the authors, except for the inclusion of brief quotations in a review. Requests for permission or further information should be addressed to "The Permissions Department", hopesyndreamz@optonline.net

Dumplinz Books are available at special discounts for bulk purchases, sales promotions, fund raising or educational purposes. For details, contact: Special Sales Department, Dumplinz Book Publishing, (917) 642-5549 / hopesyndreamz@optonline.net

Text Copyright © 2015 by Dumplinz Book Publishing
Illustrations Copyright © 2015 by Sky Owens
ISBN #: 978-0- 9964684-2-8
Library of Congress Control Number: 2015917561

Thank You Jehovah

Thank you Jehovah for granting me the talent to write...eyes so vibrant I'm able to see clear enough to dive inside of my own imagination, and for the ability to enable my friends, family, virtual family, and readers to see and visit with me in my world through my eyes.

We hang inside here; the other hangers & I,
but we never hang together.

You see; all of them are dazzling,
strong, and padded too.

I'm not as strong as all the rest,
I'm metal through and through.

They placed me in a box with a lot of my metal cousins. They shipped us all over the world in boxes by the dozens.

They housed us in a clothing store,
until one pleasant day...
a lady walked right up to me
and carried me away.

Brought me to the register,
where the cashier undressed me.

Dropped me in a bin,
"Oh Miss...I'll take that hanger please."

She took me home to work for her; we got there in a pinch.

My new home is this closet,
and
I've been here ever since.

I've watched folks grow and go away,
return with kids their own.

As time went by they'd modernize,
but they left me alone.

But now I share my home with a lot
of other fancy newer hooks.
They're cool, and I'd love to be their friend,
but they give me dirty looks.

They treat me like I don't belong,
and this was my home first.
But now this family likes them best.
That part hurts the worst.

"...when middle sister parts the doors to see what is the matter. Thinking it's the wind, she steps inside our little home... and shoves the mean ones far from me, and they leave me alone.

Their lace, cloth, frills, and padding
makes it harder for me to resist.
But I'm not that kind of hanger,
I just want a friend to hang with

I cry because I wish they'd try to know the real me deep inside. I'm a good, kind, strong, and nifty hanger of metal filled with pride.

My metal's strong {well…I think it is}, with uses quite nostalgic. When not in use I lose my sheen; that's the price of being metallic.

Winter coats, jeans, sweaters,
and dresses I would never receive.

Large padded hangers they will hire;
they hold these items with ease.

So I hang here waiting patiently
for summertime to come.
The heat brings lots of frilly clothes;
oh…
I hope they give me some.

It's middle sister's room;
a teen who changes into new outfits a lot.

Those pretty hangers she'd always use,
and her clothes I would hold…not!!

Big sister is older, more mature, and getting ready for college.
She houses no pretty hangers in her closet…to my knowledge.
Ooooh, I hope I get to leave my home and go with her for certain.
My frame is thin, so packing me in…her case won't be a burden.
They think I can't do it; think I'm weak, but I'll show them.
I've lots of strength that doesn't show…mainly from within.

All I have to do is wiggle myself
to the center from this corner.
So when she opens the closet door,
she'll see I'm right here for her.

I'll twist, slide, clink, glide, and move myself
all the way to the middle.
So when she comes to this closet, she'll see
I'm ready; fit as a fiddle.

It's almost fall and older sister is getting ready to pack.
And the middle sister is gifting pretty hangers from her rack.
Sweet middle sis hands her the blue and white spotted hanger first.
Then the yellow, red, orange, and green...oh this is getting worse.

The older sister stops her, handing most of the hangers back.

"I don't really have that much room for these hangers when I pack."

Little sister looked very sad;
she just wanted to help out.
"Awww come on now little sis,
there is really no need to pout."

"But you don't have any pretty hangers,
and I wanted to share," said little sis pouting.
"I just want you to know that I care."

"Awww sis I know you do, but I'm not going away for good.

And if I needed all these hangers, I would take them...
I would."

"So I'll tell you what I'll do my love,
I'll take me just a few.
The spotted, green,
white, red of course,
and this wired one too."

"The wired one?!"

shouted little sister,
and ran right over
to see.
"I had a wire
hanger?

Uh-Uh!!!

Who put
this here...

not me!"

The other hangers were jealous,
because older sis picked me proud.
As she raised me off the rack,
the others bitterly clanged aloud.

But I didn't care, cause' for once
in a long time someone wanted me.
And she'd never try to dispose of
me just because I was flimsy.

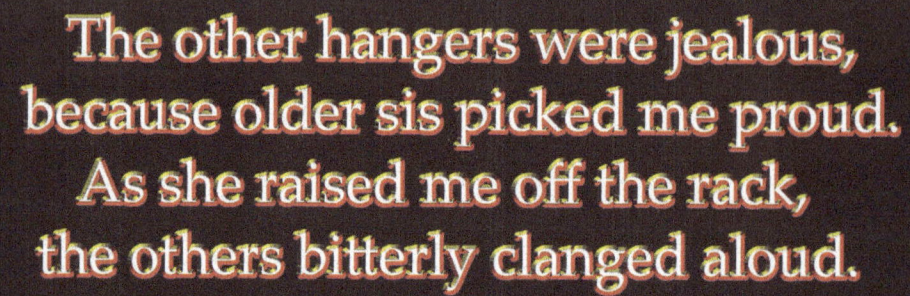

Little sister began to shout,
"That hanger is way too weak,
From the weight of all your winter clothes, it'll buckle underneath!!"

"Here!" she said. "I'll throw this in the trash my sis, and get you a nice one.
One I'm sure will be sturdy for my sis, and truly get the job done."

We walked back to her room with haste,
as she packed the rest of her stuff.
She placed a large sweater on my back,
I can do this…..I am tough.

My shoulders ached from the weight of it,
but I could never let her see.
I had to prove my strength to young sis,
the hangers, but mostly to me.

I held that sweater all the way up to college... that much was quite true.

Older sis was giving me a chance; and I was determined to see it through.

We arrived to her dorm, and inside the closet was a glowing white night light. I was so overjoyed I could have cried; now I will not be afraid at night.

But then her roommate came in the room, with lots of bags to unpack.
And as they got acquainted, she placed her hangers on the rack.

All of her hangers were very pretty, largely padded and colorful too.
When I saw all of those pretty hangers, I wanted to cry... wouldn't you?

As she placed them on the other side, to themselves they all began to giggle, The more pretty hangers she placed on the rack, the more I began to wiggle.

Her side was filled then she saw me and said, "Oh wow, a wire hanger hun?"

You really don't plan on using that thing; please tell me it's just for fun?"

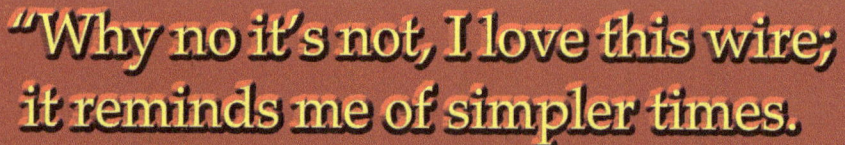

"Why no it's not, I love this wire; it reminds me of simpler times. Like when mom and dad bought thrift store clothes that always fit just fine."

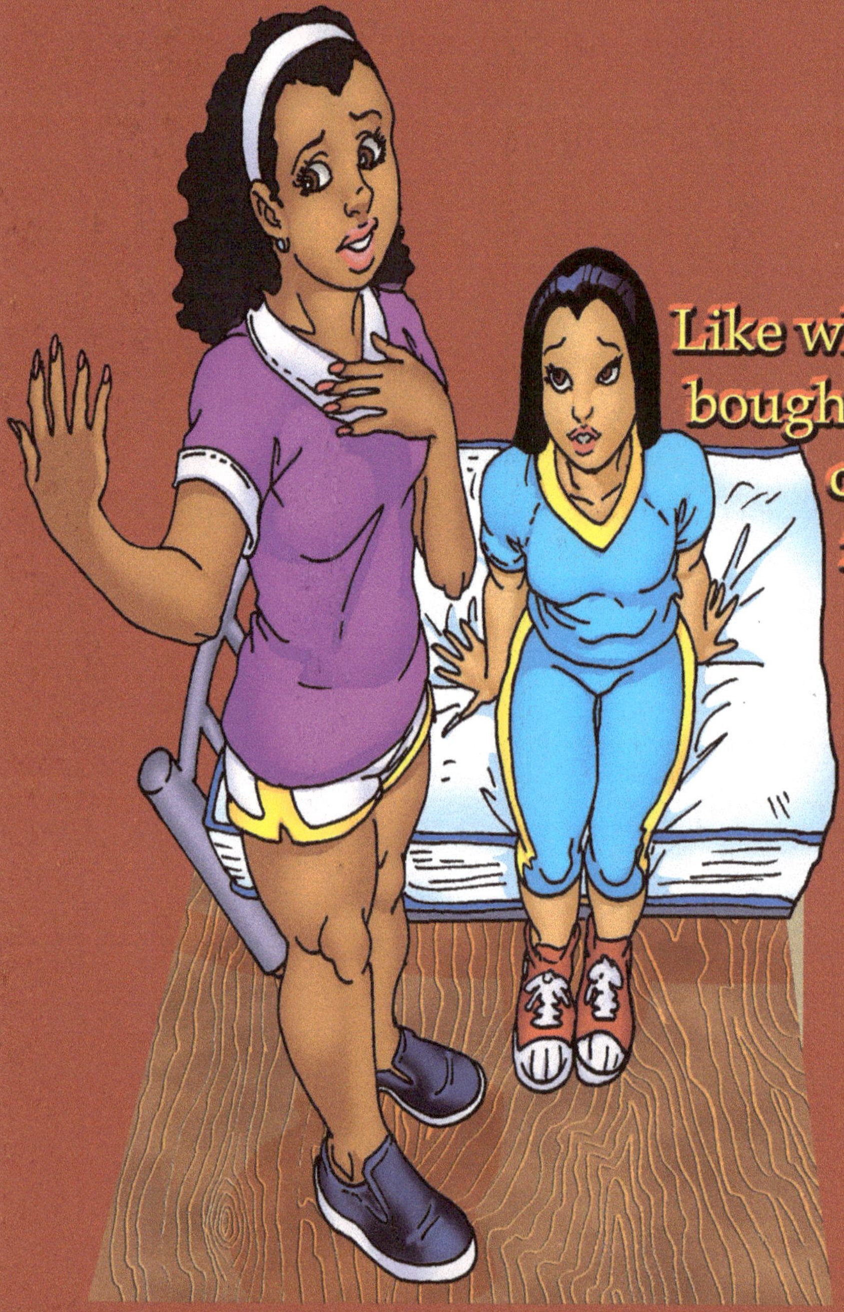

"It reminds me of that crazy car door lock that always made mom shout. And that oh so faithful wire hanger that would always help us out."

The other hangers listened and the roommate did as well. It made my heart feel warm, and my metal eyes began to swell.

I remember those good times, I remember them like yesterday. Now I know why she was so determined not to throw me away.

"Let's get some lunch and talk so I can get to know you better." She looked at me, smiled a smile, and gently removed the sweater.

The weight she took from off my back left me swaying wild and free, I didn't care about the waves; I'm not useless...now they see...me.

So when you see a wire hanger being shoved all the way to the end...

walk right up stand by their side, every wire hanger needs a friend.

See Ya Later........

Acknowledgment

    Quite often I hear people say…"If I could relive my childhood all over again…I would. I loved my childhood. Life was easy and fun when I was a kid." All **too** often I hear those words, and whenever I do…I cringe. I would never return to my childhood. It was paved with abuse both mental emotional, and physical. I was bullied in every facet of my life when I was a child, and the thought of going back seems too much like torture in a very big box. Back in those days…bullies got away with being obnoxious, evil, abusive, slap happy, and rude. It was not look upon as right…but at the same time, the action of someone stopping the bullying was non-existent. At least it was in my case.

    I grew up looking over my shoulder no matter the ship that sailed my way. In my relationships, my friendships, my kinships, my acquaintanceships, my companionships, my fellowships, my hardships, and my sportsmanship, I found it difficult to trust people, or to give my all and all to any facet of understanding, since no one understood the torture I was up against every time I woke up. Bit I persevered, and loved to tell the tale. And that is exactly what I am doing right now…telling the tale. Albeit, this story is about a little wire hanger instead of a little black girl trying not to get through life with as little drama as possible…but I'm sure despite the differences in appearance…you get the gist.

Somewhere out there in this big closely knit blanket we call life…is a child crying inside. Screaming for someone ANYONE to stop this madness. Somewhere there is a child in school hating the very fabric of the brock and mortar because of the sheer punishment it carries. I am hoping this book opens doors for the silent victims of bullies. I am hoping this book sheds light on the dark days of those children prematurely sentenced to life's cruel antics. I am hoping this book prompts conversation, sparks confessions, ignites courage, invites sympathy, kindles understanding, and dishes out support on such a grand level that the word "bullying" becomes a word only uttered by bulls.

Everyone deserves a voice…
even a wire hanger.

I want to thank all of my family and friends: tangible, virtual, old, new, found, lost, gained and obtained. Thank you for always supporting me and my writing endeavors...I love you all for your stick-to-it-tive-Rebaness.

I thank all of the mothers in my life: Juanita Wheeler, Marie Polite, Shirley Madeline Owens, Julia Strand, Shirley Callaway...and in my head...Maya Angelou. I love you all, and thank you for being the strength that has allowed me to not stop, even when I felt as if all hope was lost, and I had no choice. It was the way you've nurtured me, the way you've encouraged me, the way your ways motivated me, the way you've disciplined me, and the way you've accepted me that kept me going. So to that end I say...I love you mom(s).

Thank you Peaches; my best friend, my rock, my leaning post, my pillow, and my sister for standing by me when I didn't think these books would come out this year. But due to your perseverance, patience, and constant ever vigilant pressing ahead...here we are. To my son, Carl...thanks for putting up with me during these rushed and trying times. Writing is easy for me...but planning a book signing is murder. I love you for understanding. Thank you Nikki, Ibaria, Wheeler for being the fantasia that flourished my book signing event. Without your assistance, I would have had bare tables and naked chairs.

Thank you Chris, Tyrone, and Shauna for helping us in so many areas, I cannot begin to count. Chris Watson...thank you for assisting with the home situation and making it my dream home again. Tyrone Rhames - {little hamster on the wheel}...thank you for being the go to guy whenever we needed you, and for always showing up before time. Thank you. Shauna Leeks...thank you for proofreading "Hanger" for proofreading "Dad" and for helping me with all the Knick knacks in between. {Buh-budah-buh-budah buh-budah HAH}.

Thank you Carlos and Mimi for taking such great care of ResQ every time we needed a vacation and for making it possible for me to write my stories without having to doggie massage his highness every ten minutes. {Aw, who am I kidding you know I love it}. Thank you Rene for walking ResQ every time I fell behind the proverbial writer's eight ball. Thank you Steven Cheeks for repairing our home allowing me to finish the Little Hanger Book, and the "Spanglish" translation of Amo...with Rosie. Speaking of Rosie...

Thank you so very much, Roze Petalz, for coming into my life at such an important time. For being a true friend/sister and allowing your Latin flare to seemingly umbrella my books. Thank you little niece, Vanessa, for painstakingly listening to your mom recite Amo A Mi Hoodie well over five hundred times until you could literally hear the words in your dreamz. Your long suffering is immeasurable, I love you niecii.

Thank you Raphael for allowing me to have my November 14th book signing at your illustrious venue…"The Poet's Den Gallery." Thank you Alabama Dot's for catering the event. Your food…amazing, which is putting it mildly. Thank you DJ Blak for keeping the Jazz music flowing, and the old school tunes growing. Thank you Kent Murph for your photography skills, capturing each and every special moment as only you know how. Thank you Niecii Shawnie Core for helping out in each and every way possible. Your love for us is apparent, and we love you more. Thank you Oscar Jr. Fr being the spotlight in my family eye. I love you so much cousin. Thank you Cousin Bobbi for always reaching out for a new book to share with the world…your support is incalculable.

And finally…Thank you Quality Press, Amber Books Communication group, Inc., Tony and Yvonne Rose…for helping me make this dream book signing a reality. For allowing me to gather my materials and to print such a wonder set of books under your tutelage. Words could never express how much I appreciate all the time, effort, hours, and professionalism you showered upon me. Ours is a union that will never part.

I hope when you darlings have read these books, you incorporate them into your family lineage as the books you will hand down to the next generation as we did our Dick and Jane Books, our Really Rosie books, our Charlie Brown and the Peanuts gang books, and our forever loved Dr. Seuss books.

About The Team

AUTHOR: ISREBA WHEELER aka HOPE SYNDREAMZ has loved writing ever since she was in elementary school. At that time she was into poetry, and won a few poetry contests in school. Soon after, Isreba began to write stories for all of the children to read. The teachers told Isreba that her writing was over the heads of her classmates and when she got older, maybe then she should pursue writing as a career, but not now. So Isreba stopped writing...until she was an adult. Isreba joined a magazine staff for a while, but shortly thereafter connected with Illustrator Sky Owens and created Dumplinz Books.

Whenever Isreba is asked what inspired her to write children's books, she states, "Entertaining the vulnerable tiny fresh minds of our children today. Too much of life's negativity and nonsense trickles down into their bowls of cereal and they are forced to eat it up along with life's innocent lessons. I wanted to bring some morals and fun back into the eyes of these children, our children. I wanted to open up their mind's eye again, and help them recapture the essence of imagination." Isreba added, "I hope one day my children's books will inspire a child to sit me down when I am old and grey...make up a story off of the top of their heads, and tell me a story."

Isreba currently resides and works in Bronx, New York.

ILLUSTRATOR: PRESTON SKYLAR OWENS aka SKY OWENS first put crayon to paper at the tender age of 3, inspired by his mother and greatest fan. An avid fan of cartoons and comic books, he followed his passion for all of his life, working for such companies of Marvel, DC, and Dark Horse as a ghost artist, until he caught his first break as a solo artist with Fantagraphic comix, Antarctic Press, Lost Cause Production, London Night Studios until he finally self-published under Box Press and finally Action Bunny Comix. Self-taught from the beginning, he now uses the classic art methods of pencil, pen & ink, furthering his abilities with computer augmentations, bringing a new life to his illustrations. He now works and resides in a small town in New Jersey, enjoying his craft, bringing many creators' ideas to light.

www.ingramcontent.com/pod-product-compliance
Lightning Source LLC
Chambersburg PA
CBHW061931290426
44113CB00024B/2870